RORY WAGNER

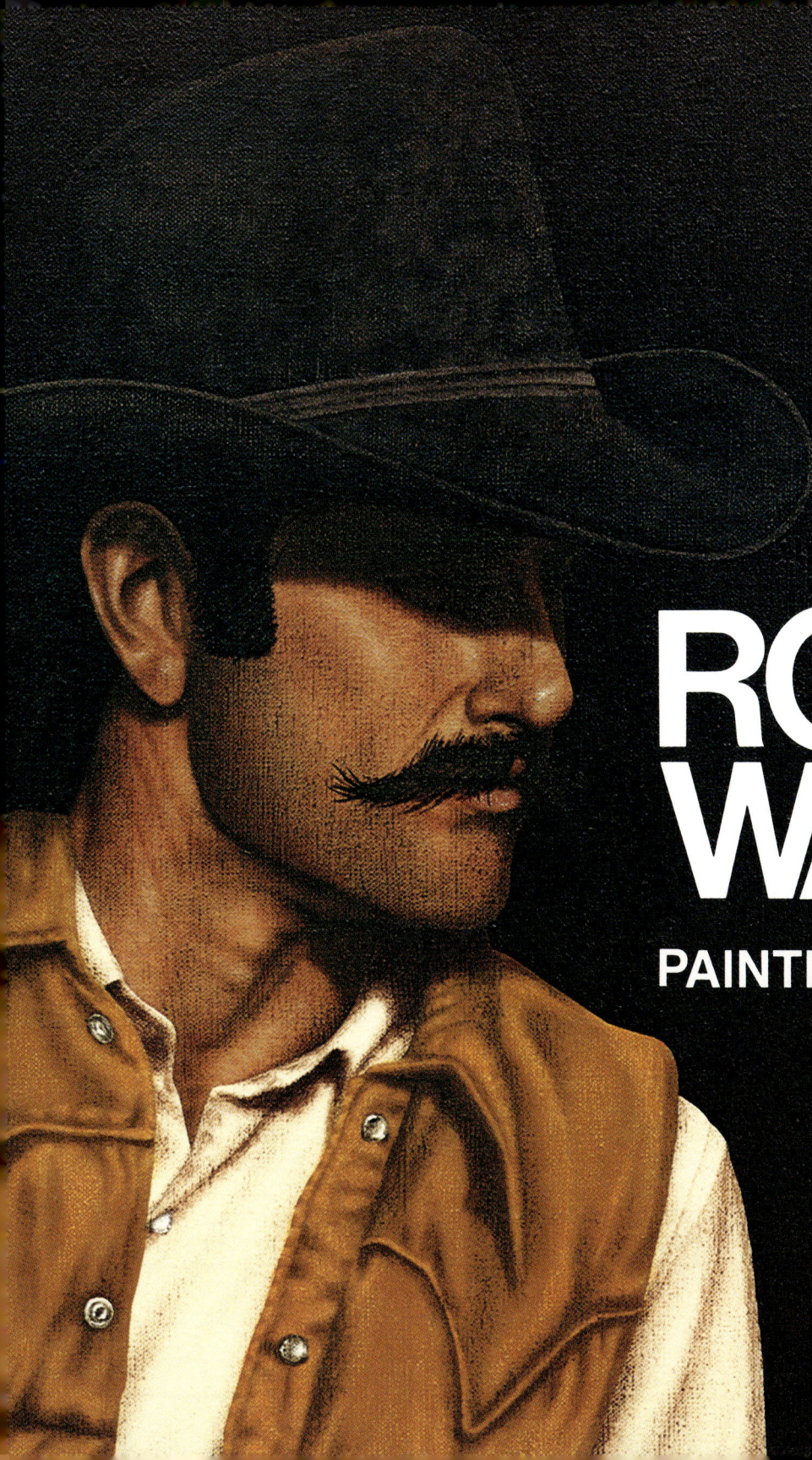

RORY WAGNER

PAINTINGS AND DRAWINGS

MARCH 27, 1982

QUAIL HOLLOW
GALLERIES
OKLAHOMA CITY

FOREWORD

Recognizing a young artist's talents has always excited me. Since establishing the Navajo Gallery in Taos, New Mexico, I have seen the work of many painters and sculptors. Several have had talent, but Rory Wagner has more than the fundamental understanding and inborn ability to do well. He has a particular style and grace, special qualities that exceed the obvious.

When we first met at the gallery in 1978, Rory was young, impressionable, and enthusiastic. He walked in off the street, lugging canvases he had hauled all the way from Florida in a very old Chrysler sedan. After looking over what he had to present, I asked him to fetch whatever else he had with him. Actually, it was more than curiosity—I had to own one!

The more of Rory's work I saw, the more I knew he would go far. He needed only the chance to paint without pressure and to exhibit with well-deserved pride. A model was hired and he started to work. His following has grown impressively in a few short years.

I've found that in life everything comes full circle. What delights me is that Rory is now encouraging and helping others appearing on the art scene.

Rory, my friend, get on with the work.

R.C. Gorman

INTRODUCTION

Living in the shadow of the Taos Mountains can be awesome for the artist with traditional aspirations. The mystique of the mountains is older even than that of the pueblos that provided the Taos founders with a lifetime of artistic sustenance. New artists arrive in and depart from this sparsely populated New Mexico community with the regularity of the seasons. One such artist, quite by accident, was captured by the mystery of the region, and discovered the wealth of artistic potential hidden within.

Rory Wagner is that artist. The intensity and quality of his paintings are electrifying. The unique style of his creations and the monumental proportions of his work command recognition, yet the viewer is given maximum consideration. Creating anatomical perfection in his subjects, Wagner floats images into almost surrealistic environments. Cowboys in skyscrapers, rodeo riders, or portraits of celebrities all typify the coherent themes that dominate his sketches and paintings. Whether dealing with the 1980s cowboy or a major portrait, his works capture a cross-section of modern America.

Painting primarily from imagination, Rory prefers to transfer his thoughts directly onto canvas. Using the acrylics he has become comfortable with, Wagner often paints from his own image to recreate body structure, muscle tone, hair fiber, or similar anatomic features. With meticulous precision, he builds up paint in layers, using the rubbing technique he developed by a most American method of trial and error. The

1

classic example of his method is "Animal Man," a 42″ x 62″ acrylic on canvas. "Many of my paintings are self-portraits. 'Animal Man' is a case in point. Containing the basic elements of my physical make-up, it presents itself as a self-portrait of my imagination," Wagner comments.

An average Rory Wagner painting requires approximately one month to create; it is seldom done in less time. In a year, he might complete a maximum of fifteen paintings. In Wagner's quest for perfection, a shirt may be repainted five or six times, a background two or three. All these changes can be followed by whiting out an entire canvas and beginning again. Rory is so particular about his works that he has even reacquired previously sold paintings in order to rework them. His dissatisfaction has sometimes caused him to take a razor blade to them to ensure their termination as a Wagner art piece. People say Ned Jacob is the most selective of contemporary American artists; Wagner must certainly equal him for honesty and integrity toward his work.

Swedish-born sculptor Kent Ullberg recently noted the "power of Wagner's portraits." Acclaim from the internationally renowned Ullberg is a typical commentary on Rory Wagner's talents. In what seems to an observer to be a stagnating New York market, one of welded I-beams and dirt-filled rooms representing art, Rory Wagner's paintings must certainly be a refreshing rarity.

Wagner has spent most of his career in relative poverty; his success might be regarded as a typical Horatio Alger story. However, Rory Wagner is anything but typical. At 31, too young for a comprehensive biography, he seems destined to succeed in an art world that has become somewhat stultified. His efforts unquestionably deserve comment.

An average Rory Wagner painting requires approximately one month to create; it is seldom done in less time.

2

THE MAN

Wagner was born in St. Petersburg, Florida, on a warm July day in 1950. His father, a highly decorated career military man, was a Maryland native; his mother's family, Rising, founded the Rising Paper Mill in Great Barrington, Massachusetts. Born into this military and socially conscious atmosphere, Rory never considered a career in art. His father believed Rory should become a world-class athlete; Rory's early childhood sketches were merely the result of adolescent boredom.

Wagner describes some of his youthful artistic experiences: "When I was twelve years old, I drew a picture of Rip Van Winkle. I drew him just as he was waking after his prolonged sleep, and included a stretch and a yawn. Very long fingernails, as I remember. I gave it to my teacher, who proceeded to enter it in one of those class art contests you see everywhere. I won the damned thing. Big deal! There must be thousands of people out there with the same dubious honor bestowed upon them at some point in their lives. I think I realized the relative unimportance of the feat at the time, because although I continued to draw, filling my text books with drawings, I never entered another contest." Throughout his school years, he left a legacy of text books containing what would today be a fortune in Wagner drawings.

By the time he reached high school, Rory was an individualist and an athlete, but still not an artist. He considered competing in the regional Olympic swimming trials, but soon decided he was lacking in dedication when he saw his opponents with their body hair shaved and their ears taped back to reduce drag in the water. Rory acknowledged that he was liter-

3

ally over his head in competition; he was never able to fulfil his father's expectations of becoming a world class athlete.

After high school, he entered the University of Florida, along with many of his friends, and continued to fill textbooks with his drawings. Little interested in school, he soon was negatively distinguished by failing everything. He could not seem to find his slot in life. Disillusioned, Rory left the university, returned home, and became involved briefly with a girl he had known in high school. He soon discovered that he needed wider horizons to explore. "I asked my father for a plane ticket to Spain, where my uncle was busy writing and having a ball. I didn't stop to consider that he might not need me to share it all with. So off I went."

If high school and college were disappointments for Rory, Europe was positively disastrous. After being in Europe only a few days, Wagner was hit one morning with the realization that he was nearly broke and several hundred miles away from Spain and the security of his uncle. Practically penniless after a dining extravaganza with a couple of resourceful young airline stewardesses, Rory was reluctant to contact his parents for money. He set off for Spain, hitchhiking when necessary, riding the train when he could afford the ticket.

Upon arriving on his uncle's doorstep, Rory found himself once more at loose ends. "I did nothing but hang around, make myself a total pain to my uncle, and write home for money." Eventually wearing out his welcome, Rory departed for home. His return was a brief one; Rory decided that it was time to grow up, and he wanted to do that in Europe. As he says, he left ". . . with eyes a bit wider open, and certainly more mature. This trip wasn't quite the disaster of the previous one." He lived in Deya del Mallorca for some time, and then in London.

When he tired of exploring the continent, he once again returned to America. But, rather than joining his family, he joined the Army. The Army helped him solve a myriad of problems, and although his performance was somewhat lacking, he had time to decide on his next step in life.

Returning to college after his military tour, Rory majored in English Literature; he finally seemed to be getting it all together. This trip to school was better for many reasons, and he

He set off for Spain, hitchhiking when necessary, riding the train when he could afford the ticket.

4

One day, out of the blue, a friend offered him fifty dollars for a charcoal drawing.

even found the time and stamina for art to become important. Although he considered it beyond belief that anyone could actually make money doing something he really enjoyed, Rory pressed on with his drawings. "Due to the old American work ethic, I'd always assumed a person had to do something he utterly hated in order to make a buck. I'd always lived by that axiom, doing really gritty jobs all my life." One day, out of the blue, a friend offered him fifty dollars for a charcoal drawing. Drawing with charcoal was a favorite pastime, and he had done this on canvas many times before. Astounded, he took the money and never again returned to college classes. He spent twenty-four hours pondering the implications of becoming the professional artist he felt compelled to be. The struggle within awakened the young man's artistic sensitivities and unleashed an energy he had not known he possessed.

5

EVOLUTION OF AN ARTIST

Europe had brought him closer to the world of art, and in doing so, shaped his future. Many hours had been spent investigating the various museums of the continent. In Paris, Rory stood in awe before enormous works of the great masters. "I always enjoyed the larger-than-life canvases and sculptures that required people to lean back and tilt their heads skywards to observe. Even today in western American art [I feel that] the important pieces are major works by William R. Leigh, Thomas Moran, Albert Bierstadt, and others. I can never paint small, possibly because I can't think in minute details. When someone looks at my work, I expect them to have to use their minds, placing themselves into the painting or seeing images and parts that intrigue them. Whether their criticism is positive or negative is of little importance. Knowing that my work promotes the thought processes and demands attention for a few brief moments is the pinnacle of my success."

Rory began his creative career by moving to Baltimore, where he thought the art world thrived. He became involved with a stable young woman; her support allowed him the time to develop as a painter. He now could concentrate one hundred percent of his time and energy on his work. And work he did, from morning until night. He was constantly seeking a formula for a saleable product, as well as refining his technique.

"I taught myself to paint; I'm still doing that. It was no easy feat without benefit of a guide of any sort. My drawing was good, which made the approach to painting easier. I attended only one drawing class in my life, but I can draw very nearly perfectly. I don't know what a degree in art would have done to that. Perhaps destroyed the inborn talent entirely. I don't know. I've seen it happen."

Lacking a solid grounding in technique, Rory began by drawing with great accuracy. "I first started painting in oils. I attempted to make my renditions realistic. That was to become an insurmountable task. A very complex thing, painting; I found out rather quickly that I would never achieve anything with my hurry-up attitude." He continued his drawing on canvas and cheap paper, while laboriously poring over books on master painters, trying desperately to figure out how they accomplished such amazing effects with a pigment-laden brush.

Vermeer served as the first guide in Rory's quest to duplicate the luminescent effects he saw in the masterpieces he studied. He spent two years layering oils onto canvas, trying to capture the essence of light and texture visible in Vermeer's work. "And that's how I learned . . . mainly through trial and error. A hell of a lot of error." Works by other masters would follow in his succession of studies, yet Rory always felt his best training was in totally duplicating the work of Vermeer.

"I had a brief fling with abstraction, but wasn't satisfied with it because I was hung up on realism. I believed rendering things in a realistic manner to be an insurmountable task. I had always drawn with a fanatic realism, extremely detailed, and naturally wanted to paint the same way. So I struggled along for years, cursing myself for my stupidity and realistic bent. I spent hundreds of hours trying to copy masterworks literally, hoping to learn their technique. I probably never did learn the right way, but I succeeded in developing a technique I shall call my own."

Rory was not happy with the nature of oil paints. While they respond with flexibility in mixing, thinning, and flowing, they are slow to cure and smear easily. After five years of experimenting with them, he eventually turned to acrylics.

During this entire experimental period, Rory was supported by a woman who totally believed in him. "I don't think she realized the time involved, but once committed, she never pulled back, even when I had the utter audacity at one point to

Rory painted primarily at night when it was cooler; in the heat of the day he slept on the floor on a blanket.

He had no money, no fame, no self-esteem . . . he was frustrated with everything and everybody.

8

move out on my own. Off I went, and with all my money rented a seventy-dollar-per-month apartment in the heart of Balti-more. I lived on the top floor of a tenement building, without a stick of furniture or any other human accoutrements aside from my pencils, paint brushes, and a few art books. I lived quite a spartan life, but it didn't really bother me because I was doing what I wanted to do. And that makes up for a world of discomfort. In fact, I was rather happy. My entertainment came from the streets below and the people who inhabited them. Fascinating. It was quite an education. I learned that life is not keen for many people. I saw fights and killings and brawls and shooting, and a total hostility that was mind-boggling. I can't begin to tell you of my fear and fascination."

He was then fully involved in his career, living on his own in a one-room firetrap. During the summer, the heat was unbear-able. Rory painted primarily at night when it was cooler; in the heat of the day he slept on the floor on a blanket. In those days, according to Rory, his work was terrible. "My techniques were not refined. I was, though, selling my work, for about one hun-dred dollars each, at a nearby gallery."

He still had trouble existing on his own, and this precari-ous life came to an end after a few months. "So back I crawled to my girlfriend, who only hesitated a few minutes before con-senting to take me in again. A truly remarkable girl. And I guess my father believed in me as much as she did, because he started sending me one hundred dollars a month to help with the bills. What a relief that was! The man was not particularly fond of artists, politicians, or actors. He lumped them all into a single derogatory category. This was quite a sacrifice for him."

At the end of his fifth year of struggle in Baltimore, Rory reached the conclusion that his career was not moving; he was desperate. He had no money, no fame, no self-esteem. He had failed to achieve even the basics of a self-sustaining existence. Irritable and impossible to live with, he was frustrated with everything and everybody. His companion finally reached the limit of her endurance and threw him out. Wagner didn't realize that these hard five years had given him the basic understanding of the subjects of his future paintings. Now, after long hours of study, he could execute the imprint of life on an aging face, knowing the reasons for the lines of concern and despair. His "dead end," as he considered Baltimore, proved to be the catalyst for his journey west.

With three hundred dollars in his pocket, Rory headed west with the intention of going to Scottsdale, Arizona, to meet Erskine Caldwell, a best-selling author whose wife was a friend of Rory's mother. Little did he know that he would never make it all the way to Scottsdale, nor that he was soon to meet a man who would change not only his perspective, but assist him in focusing his aspirations.

He did, however, make his way as far as Santa Fe, New Mexico, and was awestruck by the place. He considered taking up residence there, but was advised by a well-meaning gas station attendant that there were few cheap apartments; an abundance of hungry artists filled the few that did exist. He was sent north along the low road to Taos.

"So off I went to the north and Taos, under the tutelage of a gas station attendant. The man must have either been a genius or a telepath, or both. He knew exactly what I needed. From the first ten minutes after arriving in Taos to the present day I have had nothing but luck and good fortune. So much so that I'm very superstitious about this place. I'll probably never leave."

Traveling north, Rory was thrilled as he journeyed past the Santa Fe Opera and on to Camel Rock, Nambe, Española.

Traveling north, Rory was thrilled as he journeyed past the Santa Fe Opera and on to Camel Rock, Nambe, Española. Finally, he ascended into the mountain region. He was amazed by the clouds and the tapestries the land and mountains made as they rose and fell together in an endless hue. He didn't realize that this road had been traveled by many of the great artists of the early twentieth century. He didn't know that Blumenschein had sat on the edge of the high road painting the landscape, or that Sharp, Berninghaus, Gaspard, and others had traversed these hills to reach the pueblos and capture history in their own works. These were only names to Rory; however, his lack of knowledge about these men didn't minimize the importance of this event in his life.

Arriving in the middle of the summer season, Rory met with his first stroke of luck—he landed a cheap apartment. An astounding feat, according to anyone living in Taos. Even so,

"The gallery was the Navajo Gallery and the woman was Virginia Dooley."

Being represented by Gorman is a many-faceted thing, to say the least.

10

he was down to his last fifty dollars and realized he needed to work if he was going to pay the second month's rent, not to mention buy food and other essentials. "About a week after I moved into my new house, I wandered into a small adobe gallery on a side street called Ledoux. I liked the serene atmosphere of the place and the professionalism of the woman behind the desk. The gallery was the Navajo Gallery, and the woman was Virginia Dooley. I looked around for a few minutes until the woman asked if she could help. I said yes, that I was looking for a gallery to represent my work. She told me those decisions were up to the painter, R. C. Gorman, who owned the gallery and was the primary exhibitor there. She told me that if I could run home and get a few canvases to show, Mr. Gorman would be there in a few minutes to take a look."

Rory went to his house, gathered up five paintings, and literally threw them into his car. "They were nudes, dramatic studies of anatomy which I felt comfortable doing at the time." Back on Ledoux Street, he met a man with a multi-colored headband. "He looked at my work and inquired if I had any additional paintings, which quickly sent me packing for more. When I returned, several people were discussing my paintings."

In a situation like this, Rory's nerves usually get the best of him, but he felt comfortable with this exotic man. Gorman accepted the work and agreed to represent Rory. Being represented by Gorman is a many-faceted thing, to say the least. "My life became a whirlwind of activity. All my time was spent meeting people and going to parties and hyping myself under his guidance. I had almost instantaneous success. I went from nothing to everything in about a week. It strains the imagination, even in retrospect."

Rory was still unaware of the story of the Taos art colony, initiated by Ernest Blumenschein and Bert Phillips in 1889. Blumenschein discovered Taos when he delivered a broken wheel to a blacksmith there to be repaired. He was captivated. Rory didn't realize that just a few hundred feet away was Blumenschein's home or Walter Ufer's studio. Later he would meet American painter, Ned Jacob, who in 1960 rented Ufer's old studio. He was still unaware that he would cross the path of

Andrew Dasberg or Georgia O'Keeffe. For the moment, he had met the amazing R. C. Gorman and found a gallery to represent his work, and that was enough.

Rory sold one painting in Gorman's gallery the first day, another the second day. The association with Gorman became more intense. Not only was R. C. Gorman selling his work, he had become a friend. Gorman is considered to be an artistic genius; his approach to art, unusual and refreshing. He is able to take a novice collector and quickly turn him into a fanatic. He made people notice Rory Wagner's art, and once they noticed, they liked what they saw. His effect on Rory's work cannot be minimized. From the beginning of their acquaintance, the two discussed many subjects and values. Gorman opened his extensive library for Rory's use. Rory was welcomed into his home and presented to his friends. Within a year's time, Wagner had offers from galleries coast to coast. He had two posters of his work published by Gorman. And most importantly, his work began to sell increasingly well nationally. It was during this first year that Rory Wagner developed the direction of his work and discovered the portraits of America as seen in the faces of western people.

It was during this first year that Rory Wagner developed the direction of his work . . .

THE ARTIST

Rory Wagner is a realist. Although he has produced works of abstraction and surrealism, he has never had a "blue period" or started an artistic movement. He attempts perfection within his own themes. "I guess I'll always be a realist, mainly a representational one who uses the human being as the primary element. No matter how many times I render the human figure, I never tire of it, nor do I feel I've ever gotten it quite right. The human figure is a complex thing in all aspects, and it never ceases to fascinate me. Fortunately, it fascinates other people as well."

The creation of a painting is a semi-mystical experience, one that is different each time. The techniques, however, remain constant. Wagner's method is best described by the artist himself. "The manner in which I paint is quite different, I suppose, although I've never bothered to ask how many painters use the technique. As far as I know, I'm the only one doing it. Since I tediously invented this method, my assumption may be correct.

"I begin a canvas by stretching it myself on a stretcher that I hand-construct. I like this because I can control everything from size to quality of canvas to tautness and texture. I then prepare the surface with a thick gesso-pigment combination, and when that dries I sand the surface to achieve the desired grain, which varies with the effect I hope to achieve with any particular idea. Sometimes I apply different things to the surface of the canvas, such as a cheesecloth or sand or paper, depending on what's running through my mind at the time. This done, I begin my sketches, right on the canvas itself. I always had trouble sketching on a separate piece of paper and then transmitting the idea onto the canvas. Working from start to finish on the canvas itself has many advantages, the main one being that I am working with what will be the final product all the way through the various stages. I get totally into my idea this way.

"Once the sketches are complete, worked out to a fine line rendering of the basic idea, I begin work with the brush. The sketches are always subject to change as the work progresses; in fact, I don't believe I've ever completed a painting exactly as it was proposed in the drawing stage. Invariably, I do all of the figurative work first. The human figure, always the focus of my painting, must work. Otherwise, the painting as a whole will never come off. The undercoat of the fleshtones is pure white. Then I apply a wash of a basic skin tone, which varies with the model. In this way, I get light going through the wash, onto the white underneath, and bouncing back out. This gives a luminescent quality. From the flat surface I go into the shading tones, working darker and darker with burnt umber and burnt sienna, raw sienna, yellow oxide, and a bit of black. All of this varies with the effect I want to achieve, whether I require deep shading or a lighter shading. The paint is applied with a brush, but I rub the paint on instead of actually brushing. In this way, I can control the depth of the paint down to minute thicknesses. This technique also enables me to keep the light reflecting from underneath. Never are even my deepest shadows completely opaque. They get dark, but always allow light to go through and bounce back again. This rubbing technique is unique to me, I assume, although I couldn't say for sure. It is hell on brushes, as it wears them down after only one or two paintings, but the effect is well worth it, for I can be as smooth or as rough as I choose with the same application of paint.

"After the deep flesh tones are rendered, I proceed to the highlights. Sometimes I rub white or off-white to create a highlight, but most often I use a pencil eraser. By rubbing the eraser until the white underpainting begins to come back out, I control how much highlight I require. If I make a mistake and rub too long or too hard, the washing with mid-skin tone must

"The human figure, always the focus of my painting, must work."

"The paint is applied with a brush, but I rub the paint on instead of actually brushing."

13

"The quality of the highlight can be manipulated by going over the surface again and again with the base color, again allowing light to bounce out from the white underneath."

be repeated and I begin again. In the case of a bright glint on any feature, such as a nose or lip, I use an opaque white.

"The flesh tones completed, I then go on to complete the figure or figures, rendering the clothing, if any. These are done in much the same manner as the figure's flesh tones. I start, for example, by painting a shirt in a mid-range color of my choice. This is a flat, opaque color brushed on in the conventional manner. Then I do the highlights by rubbing a pure white pigment where I want the highlights to appear. Once the paint is dry, I go over these white spots with the original base color of the shirt, rubbing the color over the white in a very thin coat. This requires bearing down quite a bit with the brush, and is the main cause for the demise of an expensive brush. The quality of the highlight can be manipulated by going over the surface again and again with the base color, again allowing light to bounce out from the white underneath. The shadows come next, almost exactly as described for the flesh tones, except I use the base color of the fabric in all dark tones, with burnt umber for the most part. In this way I am able to achieve a continuity of the whole.

"The figure complete, I then go on to whatever else I've in mind for the painting, moving from back to front (background to foreground). I may choose to add another figure. If this is the case, I simply overpaint the original rendering with an opaque paint to cover up what has been done previously. I do this many times, sometimes to the entire painting. Most of my canvases have at least one, and many times several, paintings underneath the one on the surface. But it is my opinion that the painting you see is the superior one. Not everyone concurs with the opinion!

"The painting complete, I proceed to the varnish. After the varnish dries, I usually apply a coat of removable matte varnish on top. Depending on the desired effect, I may not do this. Then I take the painting to the framer's to be crated and sent into the wild blue yonder. And that's that!"

Rory Wagner's position as an artist is clear. His works are meditations on human features and characteristics. All of his values, whether political, social, or aesthetic, are transferred onto canvas directly through the subjects he paints. The art-

14

ist's life experiences are often reflected in his subjects. One such painting, for example, places the twentieth-century cowboy in the foreground of a Paris street scene. Wagner was in Paris at a crucial point in his life, and found himself a young American in a new environment. His work often combines elements from his past with his vision of the future.

Wagner is neither naïve nor vain about his works. He realizes the impact of his medium and the social meanings his images impart. He is not interested in being a western artist in the style of Clark Hulings; rather, his intention is to unfold a great American drama for the viewer. He places little emphasis upon being a Taos artist. Although this is the place of his residence, it is coincidental in relation to his subjects. Rory Wagner's goals are not limited to the southwestern geographical area or western market; he attracts contemporary criticism. In this context, it is significant to note that the majority of people who collect his work are major urban buyers from New York and Los Angeles. His paintings are often part of diverse collections, hanging in many cases with the works of Fritz Scholder, Georgia O'Keeffe, and others with a modern approach to art. One interesting remark came from a California man who stated, "I have a Clark Hulings, a Tom Lovell, and two John Clymers. Now all I need is a Rory Wagner." While flattered by remarks such as this, Rory more seriously desires that his works end in important museums, respected galleries, corporate collections, and ideally, with enthusiastic art lovers who share his values.

Critical opinion regarding his work has always demanded Rory's attention; however, he does not deal with "hip pocket" criticism very well. He is personally strong-willed, abrupt, and opinionated. Compromise is no longer acceptable in his life or in his work. A popular western art dealer once suggested he simplify his style and produce a larger volume of works annually in order for more galleries to be able to promote him. Rory left the conversation in a rage. Those who discuss or inspect a Wagner painting will always be observing the finest example of his art. "Mediocrity is for Detroit car manufacturers, not my work. Although I have yet to paint a canvas that is one hundred percent by my standards, I have yet to compromise the quality

Rory Wagner's goals are not limited to the southwestern geographical area or western market; he attracts contemporary criticism.

"Mediocrity is for Detroit car manufacturers, not my work."

15

of acceptable paintings."

While it remains true that Wagner has experienced several transitional periods, the bulk of his important paintings have been done since he has come to Taos. Although he has explored new subject matter, the basic emphasis has remained constant. He has nearly abandoned drawing and sketching for sale; however, Wagner pencil drawings are highly sought after because of the detail included. His forté has always been drawing, and his paintings are an extension of this talent. An example of this may be seen on pages 17–18, with the development of the portrait, "Briseur de Coeurs." Another example is the brilliant painting, "The Warrior," page 24; it incorporates the details of the working cowboy and his saddle into a non-responsive background. The impact is a graceful blend of textures: leathers, cloth, and a felt hat integrate into the format.

The commissioned painting, "Dance of Dragons," represents the closest example of a painting which was completed to specifications. The 36″ x 72″ canvas is a difficult size on which to work. The painting was completed at the request of Barbara Mikkelsen for the Herring National Bank of Vernon, Texas. The collectors had a size requirement: they needed a piece that would fit into a prominent place in their new bank facility. They gave Wagner the freedom to choose his own subject and style. Subsequently, a second painting, "Of Noble Intent," was commissioned for the corporate collection.

Whether painting for commission or his own pleasure, Wagner's overriding concerns are quality, accuracy, and impact. His basic motivation for working on large canvases stems from his belief that a major body of work must be established in order to ensure an artistic legacy. Rory Wagner wants to become an internationally recognized artist, with paintings of substance and value to his credit. He is uncompromising in this regard. Years of poring over art books have given him a unique understanding of the nature of enduring art.

Whether painting for commission or his own pleasure, Wagner's overriding concerns are quality, accuracy, and impact.

STEP 1. Rory has gessoed an original canvas and has finished his preparatory drawing on the face of the canvas. After sketching, Rory does preliminary shading with a light burnt sienna/burnt umber mix. He than goes over the entire face like this from start to finish, gradually deepening the shadows, until a darker shadow color is needed. Darkening the shadows with a burnt umber/black mix, Rory goes over and over to keep control and graduate his shadows slowly. He is actually rubbing the pigment on with a standard brush. The dark shadows are many layers thick.

STEP 2. With most of the shading complete, the eyes are painted in with an opaque, flat grey blue. The choice of color is important here, because it must be kept in mind what the final color is to be after adding a deeper blue in the iris and shading the highlights. Detail work such as eyes and hair must be done concurrently with the rest of the painting to keep the work cohesive. Rory blocks in the eyebrows, eyelashes, mustache, and hair. He has not yet realized he will not be happy with the original drawing in which the right eye is too high and a bit too large. Often times he discovers his mistakes by default.

17

STEP 3

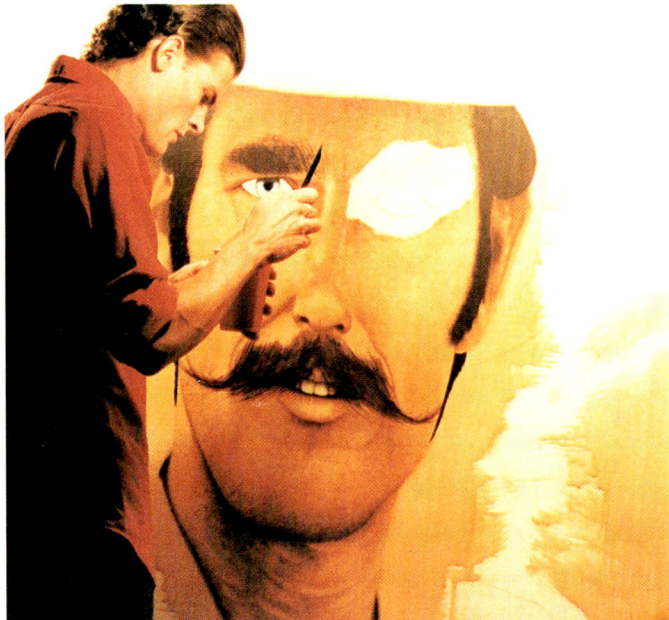

STEP 4

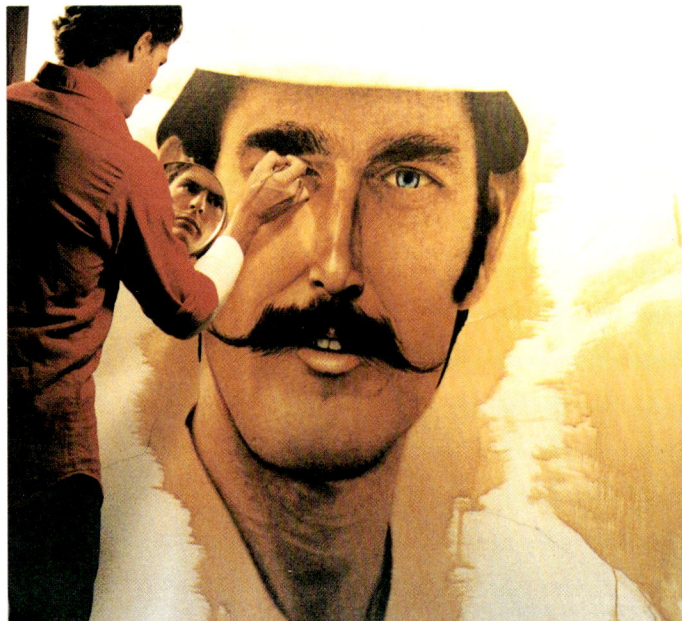

18

STEP 5

STEP 6

STEP 3. Rory comments, "Here I had completed the mustache and eyebrows and eyes, only to see something askew, not quite right, in the face. The mistake was a subtle one and therefore difficult to detect at first. I just knew that the right eye and eyebrow didn't jive with the other features, giving my model a twisted look. So I overpainted the area with the original base white and I began again, repeating every stage I had gone through before. It can be tricky to get this overpainted area to match the original painting, since I am dealing with glazes and not opaque paint. Notice that I have removed all the detail work in the left eye as well. I did this so I could better see the eyes as a pair and not individually. After staring at a painting for so many days, it's sometimes difficult to get an objective viewpoint. For this reason, I use a mirror a lot; seeing the painting in reverse establishes one's objectivity. It is often a shock to see the work in reverse, as it sometimes looks entirely different."

STEP 4. Finishing up the eyes for a second time, the shading is now different, especially on the nose and around the eyes. At this point, Rory uses his own face for a model. This process of repainting the eyes cost Rory more than three days of work.

STEP 5. After painting in the hat and background, Wagner moves toward the shirt. This took a long time because he changed his mind many times. Eventually, he redrew the area as a shirt and vest which satisfied him. Sometimes the only way to see a color is to paint it on. Rory worked on the vest and shirt before commenting: "I screwed up again. I drew in the vest, painted the shirt white, but painted the vest brown thinking to keep my hues cohesive. This didn't work so I went back to red, which was a good idea to begin with." The painting nearly complete, Wagner rubs the original red color of the vest over the white areas in thin coats. This glazing technique highlights the texture of the fabric.

STEP 6. The vest is now shaded and the final glazing is done, followed by adding details such as buttons on the vest, stitching in the fabric, and the hair. "The hair I ended up doing over three times. First I made it too long and thick, then too short and thin. Finally, I reached a compromise which can be seen in the final product. Once the painting is completed to my satisfaction, I usually let it sit around for a couple of days to be sure I like it, or that it will be successful. Next I varnish the work. After years of beating my brow over varnishing techniques—my work is so large that varnishing is a real ordeal—I use a compressor like the ones you see used to paint cars, and this works like a dream. It gives me a nearly perfect final coat to my work, and is easy to apply."

Wagner often signs his work very lightly on the front so as not to disturb the image. There is drama in every aspect of his work, and the signature is no exception. The piece is always signed and titled on the back, with the year of completion. If the finished piece is a combination of several paintings, this is also noted.

20

AMERICAN COWBOY
acrylic on canvas
46 x 50 inches
1980

AMERICAN
COWBOY

"This painting originally appeared under the same title, with the main figure wearing a flag shirt (red and white stripes, with white stars on a blue field on the yoke), and white chaps. The background was a sunset scene with mountains bordered by the black green silhouettes of trees and leaves in the foreground. I first changed the background to a skyscape of multi-hued clouds and light. That wasn't particularly successful, so I overpainted it again in an off-white (to regain a perspective of sorts). I then started changing the figure itself, painting the shirt white, then blue, then pink, and finally back to white. I then painted the chaps a more conventional brown leather color, and everything started to come together. I overpainted the background again, this time a dark, burnt umber/black. At this point, the shirt stood out too much, so I painted it a myriad of darker colors, finally opting for the deep red in the final product. The figure's hat also went through this process, starting out off-white and finally ending up a dark brown. The only thing that didn't change was the horse and tack. That was the basic element that had to remain constant."

ANIMAL MAN

" 'Animal Man' was originally a completely different painting entitled 'John Deere.' It was a portrait of a cowboy adjusting his stirrups for the bronc-riding event in a rodeo. I decided the canvas was not successful, so I sanded down the face of the canvas to get rid of the glossy texture of the varnish, and re-gessoed over the top. I did this twice to regain some texture on the surface, and completely hide the painting underneath. Some colors have a tendency to bleed up through any over-painting, so you must be careful to do this right lest you ruin another painting.

"I had the idea to juxtapose a cowboy figure, very macho, against a completely different idea of serenity and quiet. For this I used the concept of Japanese Buddhism; I painted the figure first, getting the expression and tone just right, very aggressive, confident and sexual. I then painted an animal-god figure, a stone sculpture, of the Chinese Mao-Mao-shan (opting for a Chinese symbol instead of Japanese as originally intended), which the figure was leaning against. I painted another stone god in the foreground to the right. The background was a grey stone wall—type thing. But the painting just didn't work at all. The main figure was really successful, and I was extremely reticent to scrap the entire painting. I began to rethink my intent and ideas.

"Still wanting to juxtapose the cowboy with something completely different, I painted a French storefront behind the main figure, complete with obviously French articles behind the glass, and a French logo on the glass itself. This didn't work either. But I did realize what I was doing wrong.

"The figure itself was so strong that it was carrying the

ANIMAL MAN
acrylic on canvas
42 x 62 inches
1981

23

THE WARRIOR   acrylic on canvas   26 x 44 inches   1981

24

weight of the painting as a whole, without further need of embellishment. I had my statement there, and anything else was just a needless distraction. So I decided to keep the painting simple, which would add drama to the figure itself. I painted a white board fence behind the figure with some tack hanging on it (a bridle, reins, gloves, and a man's bareback rigging for rodeo). I added a gear-bag in the foreground at the figure's feet. But again, it was too busy and just didn't look right. Somehow, I had to go much simpler and try to accentuate the main figure more.

"Frustrated, I took a walk around the ranch where I was living. When things are going badly, it is sometimes beneficial to get away and remove yourself from the object of your concern. I knew the painting could work if I found the right format, but that concept was totally escaping me. While walking, I came upon an old tack room, the wood very dark and pitted with age and use. The door to the tack room was a half-and-half with enormous black hinges. I stood there looking at it for awhile, then walked over and opened the top half. The interior was almost totally black. I figured that this would be a perfect setting for my cowboy, against that dark wood and black interior. So I went back to my studio and overpainted the background again, for the final time. And that is the way the painting now appears. A lot of people don't like this painting, have an extremely negative reaction to it; a lot of people really like it. But there is no apathy to it from anyone, which I consider successful."

THE WARRIOR

"I paint big, I always have. The only time I create a small canvas is when part of a larger one doesn't work and I cut off portions of it and restretch it. 'The Warrior' was originally a larger painting, but I cut him off at the waist. I want a big image, no matter what it is; I guess I like the drama. People are often awestruck when they walk into a room and are faced with the sheer size of my paintings."

THE FARRIER   acrylic on canvas   44 x 68 inches   1981

26

THE FARRIER

Traditionally, the farrier has been an important component of western life. A properly shod horse was a necessity. Today, the farrier still plays an active role wherever horses are used for work and pleasure.

Wagner has chosen to depict the strength and hard-working nature of this profession in "The Farrier."

"This painting is similar to most that I paint. I changed the background a few times, the hat twice, and the shirt several times. The rest was easy, a snap. It only took a month."

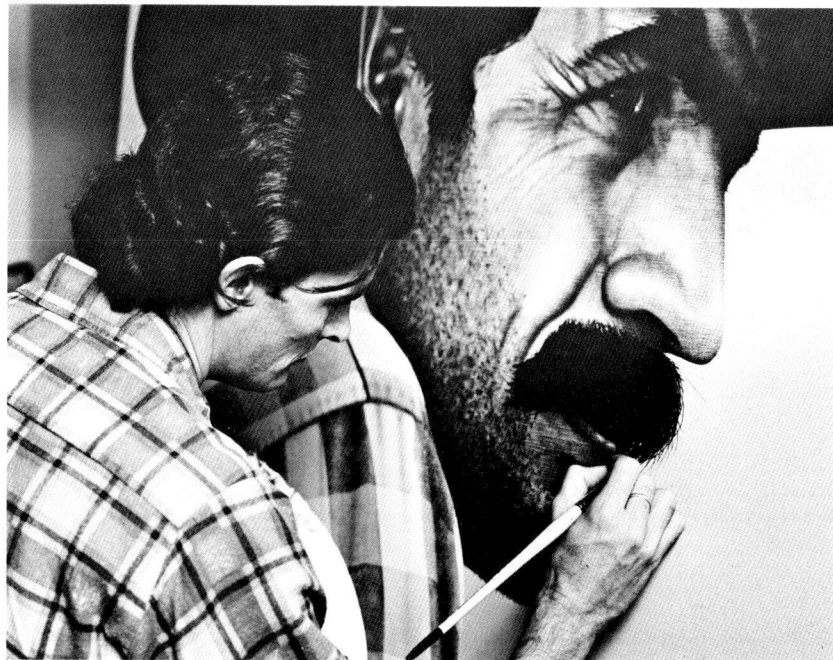

27

DANCE
OF DRAGONS

In March of 1981, Julia Black of the Taos art gallery of the same name contacted Quail Hollow Galleries to commission two paintings by Wagner for the new Herring National Bank of Vernon, Texas. Wagner seldom does commissioned work; however, he accepted because the purchaser, Barbara Mikkelsen, placed almost no restrictions or requirements on him, asking only that this painting be 36" x 72". At several points, Rory almost gave up working on this long, narrow canvas. He found the solution to the problem this size created in his surrealistic background and central figure.

"Due to the format of this work, totally foreign to my character, I had one hell of a time coming up with an idea. I pre-sketched a myriad of ideas on the canvas, many quite detailed; none worked. Then I struck on the idea of the main figure on horseback, rendered it on the canvas and went from there. Luck played a big part of this painting. I had no overall idea at all. I did paint in about three hundred cows in the background at one point, and had one more cowboy on horseback in there (which you can still see if you know where and how to look), but they eventually ran off stage left. At the end I sort of went crazy with white paint, and I really lucked out. I like the ghostly atmosphere that was created."

28

DANCE OF DRAGONS   acrylic on canvas   36 x 72 inches   1981

29

R. C. GORMAN, PORTRAIT
acrylic on canvas
72 x 68 inches
1978

30

R. C. GORMAN, PORTRAIT

The portrait of R. C. Gorman was originally conceived one evening as Rory sketched Gorman's profile on a napkin at a local Taos restaurant. R. C. proclaimed he would commission Wagner to do a portrait of him as big as the wall, pointing to a large white adobe wall in the restaurant. The portrait evolved from that night on the town.

The piece, which Gorman has shown to practically everyone visiting Taos, has been reproduced in poster form for the 1978 Rory Wagner exhibition at the Navajo Gallery, Old Town, Albuquerque. It also appears on the back cover of the book *R. C. Gorman: The Posters*, published by Northland Press, copyright 1980.

CARL

"Occasionally I will paint a very special piece for someone who has helped my career. I took great pride in completing this portrait of Carl Gorman, one of the famous Navajo code talkers, for R. C.'s birthday. This is a companion piece to the portrait I did of R. C. The painting was an incredible struggle. I repainted it three times, twice on the same canvas. R. C. Gorman displays this prominently over his fireplace in his home in Taos."

CARL
acrylic on canvas
72 x 68 inches
1980

33

34

CAT AMONG
THE PIGEONS
acrylic on canvas
66 x 70 inches
1981

CAT AMONG
THE PIGEONS

Probably one of the most dramatic works by Wagner, "Cat Among the Pigeons" is a large canvas with an unusually effective color mix. The sky gives power and dignity to this western depiction of a ranch hand caught in a ring of cattle as the day draws to a close.

"This work was painted over another finished painting I didn't like. I tried a new technique here in that I adhered a layer of cheesecloth to the whole surface of the canvas. I do things like this on a whim. I liked the effect, although it's the last time I ever tried it. I had some problems with the head of the main figure, changing it entirely two or three times. I also had painted all the cows red at first, but opted in the end to include a couple of Angus."

36

SIMMS, State I
six-color stone lithograph
22½ x 30½ inches
1981

SIMMS

Using a grease pencil, Wagner works directly on a block of Bavarian limestone to produce a highly detailed drawing. The original drawing had been selected by Peter Holmes of Origins Press, Tubac, Arizona, and Wagner as suitable for the intricate lithography printing process. Wagner felt he needed to produce an affordable work that would be more generally available to the public, since he does so few paintings. Lithography gives him the opportunity to meet this need while maintaining the quality he demands of himself.

As he explains, "The nature of my work really doesn't lend itself to fine art printing, so when I attempt this, it usually involves working extra hours to produce a workable drawing. 'Simms' was no exception, requiring five weeks of my attention to produce."

The success of this piece has broadened Wagner's collector base and increased his reputation as a multi-talented artist.

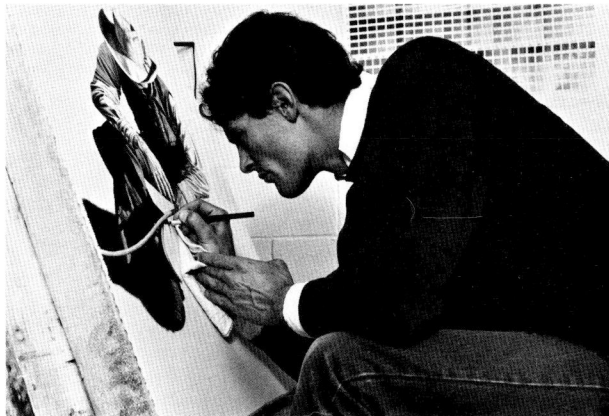

37

BRISEUR
DE COEURS

"The color scheme of a painting sometimes is arrived at by trial and error. Often times I must overpaint many, many times to get everything off. This consumes most of my time, these decisions. I sit for hours staring at the canvas, trying to visualize the colors I want to use for the various areas, and trying to decide on the correct paint values. Quite often I get an idea, paint it, and if it doesn't work, go through the whole process all over again. This is especially true of this painting. The shirt was never quite what I wanted, so I experimented with the idea of a vest and shirt. Then I changed the color of the vest; eventually, I wound up painting it the color I had chosen for it the first time. The face, of course, also consumes a great deal of time. I painted it first, getting the skin tones right. Then I found that one eye was slightly out of line. In order to correct this, I painted out the entire right eye as well as the detail work in the left eye so that I could see them as a pair. It's usually easier to get the correct perspective that way."

38

BRISEUR DE COEURS
acrylic on canvas
56 x 60 inches
1981

40

TEN-FIVE
acrylic on canvas
68 x 48 inches
1980

TEN-FIVE

"This painting went well for me from start to finish. Easy, in fact! I had no major problems, except for the cow in the foreground, which I painted twice. The second cow was a favorite of mine whom I named Barney Bubnash; he died a sudden death of unknown causes one afternoon. Quite heartbroken, I included him in the painting. I have immortalized young Barney, who deserved no less."

"Ten-Five" received overwhelming acceptance at the 1980 National Finals Rodeo in Oklahoma City. Over 100,000 people viewed this large work at the Quail Hollow Galleries rodeo exhibition. Three Wagner paintings were included in the show which also included other nationally important artists. A former rodeo calf roper turned bank officer purchased this piece for his office.

42

FERAL MAN   acrylic on canvas   36 x 72 inches   1981

FERAL MAN

Wagner's basic concept of the working cowboy may be best illustrated by the 1981 painting, "Feral Man." It illustrates as well Wagner's flexibility and his talent as a full-figure portrait artist. This typical scene from a nearby Taos ranch was recreated from Rory's memory.

44

POINT OF REFERENCE
acrylic on canvas
58 x 52 inches
1981

POINT
OF REFERENCE

"This painting goes a bit astray from convention, as I am wont to do occasionally. The cowboy is a friend of mine whom I've painted many times. The little jar to the right is actually a Syrian athlete's flask, circa A.D. 1–400. Its mottled coloration is due to corrosion and age. Notice that the flask is painted in a completely different perspective than the rest of the painting —I'm reluctant to explain the reason for this. I'll let the viewer try to decipher my meaning.

"At one time, I had painted in a blue doorway to the right of the figure, and an ancient marble statue of a Chinese lion on the floor. . . . It didn't work. I then rendered a Pi disc (a large rose jade wheel) in lieu of the lion. That didn't work either. I finally ended up with a simple and what I believe to be a quite effective flask. Its coloration is accurate, although I made it a bit larger than it really is.

"One thing that is probably not obvious is the texture of the varnish. I purposely mottled it to make it look weathered and old, to further accentuate the ancient flask. When viewing the painting up close, this becomes evident. The scribbling at the bottom of the painting is my signature in Japanese."

UNTITLED DRAWING

This dramatic black-and-white work demonstrates Rory Wagner's versatility most clearly. The way in which he has chosen to develop a positive/negative ambiance through the use of stark tones and foreshortening will affect each person who sees it differently.

While Wagner feels that the cowboy and the West represent the heart of America, he is not limited to strictly western subjects. Wagner's art captures the essence of modern man—strong, self-assured, self-contained—regardless of his lifestyle.

UNTITLED DRAWING
pencil with acrylic wash
25 x 36 inches
1981

47

MAN FROM TAOS   acrylic on canvas   48 x 56 inches   1981

48

MAN FROM TAOS

Wagner often utilizes a black background to add definition and drama to his subjects: "Man from Taos" is a case in point. Painting in this style is even more difficult than working into backgrounds. Negative space requires greater attention to primary focal points; in addition, the entire subject must be painted to reflect the luminous quality of the figure.

After five weeks of work on this painting, Wagner comments: "Nothing to it; I changed the shirt a few times before adding a vest which finally solved the problem. I painted the hat twice and the background changed a bit, in fact, many times before I opted for the black in the final product. Changing the color of a background usually throws a painting off, and things must be altered accordingly. When a background goes from light to dark, many things on the figure don't quite fit any more, including the flesh-tones. It can be a real hassle, and very time consuming."

MAN FROM TAOS
preliminary
pencil drawing
22 x 30 inches
1981

49

OF NOBLE INTENT

This work represents the second of two paintings commissioned by Barbara Mikkelsen of Vernon, Texas. She required one finished action painting, and "Of Noble Intent" filled her need admirably. Actually, it is a very popular image. Many people wanted to purchase this prior to it being crated. This is a typical problem with Rory's works—they are so large that they are impossible to hide while awaiting shipment. Probably half of the people on the two-year waiting list for his work have been influenced by paintings they could not have.

50

OF NOBLE INTENT   acrylic on canvas   56 x 68 inches   1981

AFTERWORD

In late October of 1978, I travelled to Taos, New Mexico, to meet with Virginia Dooley, director of the Navajo Gallery. The purpose of the trip was to consummate an arrangement for R. C. Gorman to have a one-man showing at the Quail Hollow Galleries in Oklahoma City. The trip proved to be quite productive. I found Virginia Dooley to be very helpful in arranging the art show; not only was she experienced in planning and developing the schedule and criteria for our gallery to achieve, but she was instrumental in suggesting that we handle Gorman's show posters to help build enthusiasm with new collectors. As an afterthought, she included a poster of Gorman. I was immediately struck with this poster—he was captured in profile, his long flowing hair trimmed with a brightly colored scarf that had been fashioned into a headband. The total effect was striking, yet the artist's signature intrigued me the most, as it was one of those which could not be read.

Within a few minutes, my curiosity got the best of me and I asked Virginia who had done this handsome portrait. She led me to the north wall of the gallery to view two additional paintings by the same artist. These were quite large nudes; the figures were perfectly rendered and beautifully displayed the talents of the artist. Virginia finally told me that his name was Rory Wagner, a discovery of Gorman's and one of the gallery's most important assets. My first impulse was to ask when I could meet Wagner and begin handling his work. Upon a moment's reflection, I decided to table the matter. I had my hands full with the Gorman program just then, and I knew I would be making many more trips to Taos over the coming months. Wagner would have to wait.

My next trip to Taos was in August, 1979. I was greeted by Gorman at his gallery. He was busy with the finishing touches on a nude male drawing. His model stood motionless a few feet away. On the far wall hung a portrait of R. C. Gorman, the original of the posters I had received on my previous trip. As if drawn by the artistic energy displayed, I approached this magnificent painting. I later observed other people walk by the painting and experience the same sensation.

I finally met Rory Wagner later in the day while dining at Casa Cordova, in the shadow of the Sangre de Cristo mountains. He turned out to be a twenty-eight-year-old artist with a warm personality and a loud laugh. We covered many topics of conversation that evening, but his work was not among them. I was delighted to meet this young man, casually dressed but firm of conviction. We talked and became friends.

It was eight months before Quail Hollow received any of Wagner's work.

It was eight months before Quail Hollow received any of Wagner's work. In March, 1980, the day of our long-awaited Gorman show finally arrived, and many important ingredients flowed together simultaneously. We received our first painting from Wagner, a portrait of a cowboy stationed in front of a rodeo stall gate. About twenty minutes after the piece was uncrated, an Oklahoma City oil man purchased it. In addition, he asked for the first right to see each piece we received prior to displaying the work. Fortunately, I was able to make it clear to him that Rory Wagner did too few paintings for this to be possible.

Eighteen hundred people came to see Gorman during the two days of our opening. He performed like a pro, entertaining collectors in his inimitable style. We had guests from at least twelve states, as far away as Hawaii. Rory's painting was hanging in an out-of-the-way area of the gallery, yet it did not escape continuous attention.

Rory's painting was hanging in an out-of-the-way area of the gallery, yet it did not escape continuous attention.

Mr. and Mrs. John Hazleton attended the Sunday opening of Gorman's show. Unlike most people, they had come to see if we had any of Rory Wagner's works. They knew of the friendship between Gorman and Wagner, having met Rory a few months previous in Taos. Since the time of their introduction to Rory, they had purchased three of his paintings. They were elated to find that we were exhibiting his work, but disappointed that they were a day late to purchase it. Had we been fortunate enough to have five paintings on hand at the time, the Hazletons would have purchased them all, so great is their enthusiasm for his work.

After the Gorman show, I established a working relationship with Rory, which includes handling his original works and lithographs. In December, 1980, Wagner led Quail Hollow Galleries' exhibition at the National Finals Rodeo held in Oklahoma City. All three of his paintings were sold and several commissions came as a result of the exhibition. At present, I have nearly thirty people waiting for the next painting Rory Wagner produces.

Wagner's work was reviewed by *Southwest Art* magazine in an article by Tricia Hurst in October, 1981. His work has been published in stone lithography by Origins Press of Tubac, Arizona, and he has been selected to complete both an album and book cover in 1982.

Over the coming years, Rory Wagner will certainly be the subject of many critical evaluations. Although he is young, his work has already attracted the attention of many private and corporate collectors. The future will surely unfold the talents of this young man upon the American art scene. The paintings presented in this book represent an introduction to one of the Southwest's most respected new artists.

MICHAEL WIGLEY
March, 1982

Over the coming years Rory Wagner will certainly be the subject of many critical evaluations.

54

ART INDEX

PHOTOGRAPHIC CREDITS

Gordon Adams, Taos, New Mexico pp. 24, 26, 39, 42, 47, 49
David Cobb, Creative Resources, Oklahoma City, Oklahoma
pp. 20, 29, 34, 40, 48
Navajo Gallery, Taos, New Mexico p. 30